2595810

Bibliographica Judaica 5

A Bibliographical Series of
The Library of Hebrew Union College-
Jewish Institute of Religion
Edited by Herbert C. Zafren
Professor of Jewish Bibliography

How <u>Do</u> You Spell Chanukah?

A General-Purpose Romanization of Hebrew for Speakers of English

by Werner Weinberg

Cincinnati, Hebrew Union College Press, 1976

Standard Book Number: ISBN 0-87820-903-4
Library of Congress Catalog Card Number: 74-82492

Contents

7   Foreword

9   To the Reader

10   Romanization Table

12   Basic Terms and Assumptions

13   Some Specific Problems of English

14   The Existing Hodgepodge

15   Earlier Attempts at Unification

16   Standardization Can Be Achieved

17   Uses and Users

18   Some Principles of a General-Purpose Romanization

19   Detailed Considerations

19   Homophones

19   *Alef* and *Ayin*

21   *ch* versus *kh, h* and *h*

22   *ts* versus *tz*

22   Digraphs

23   *a, e, i, o, u*

23   *ei* (or Perhaps *é*) for *Tsere*

24   Indicating the *Shva*

25   The Endings *-ah, -eh* and *-oh* versus *-a, -e* and *-o*

26   *ai* (also *oi* and *ui*)

26   No Need for Doubling Letters

27   No Reason to Hyphenate Prefixes to the Word

28   Capitalization

30   Will Options and Exceptions not Further Disunity?

31   Reading Rules

31   Ashkenazic Hebrew

32   A More Exact System

33   Foreign and International Words

36   Annotated Samples

37   *Kadish*

39   *Ve'ahavta*

40   *Hatikvah*

41   *Maoz Tsur*

42   *Yerushalayim Shel Zahav*

42   A Hebrew Lesson

43   Concerning the Word Lists

46   General Word List

54   Special Word Lists

54   The Alphabet

54   The Vowel Points

54   The Jewish Months

54   Holidays, Festivals, Fasts

55   The Books of the Bible

55   The Weekly Torah Portions

56   The Mishnah or Talmud Tractates

Foreword

Some years ago, I faced, as a librarian, the question of utilizing the computer for cataloging Hebrew as well as non-Hebrew books. While that question is not yet satisfactorily answered, my search for an answer led to a study of various systems of converting Hebrew to roman characters and to the realization that the state of the art of converting (or romanizing or transliterating) could only be characterized then as chaotic.

While many people had previously proposed "perfect" systems of romanization of Hebrew, Werner Weinberg systematically studied the past and developed an approach that showed eminently good sense: different systems for different purposes. His approach was vigorously adopted by the Subcommittee for Romanization of Hebrew and Yiddish of the American National Standards Institute (ANSI), Standards Committee Z-39.

The Subcommittee endorsed the romanization system that Dr. Weinberg presents in this booklet and accepted it as a general-purpose system that could be useful to laymen and to scholars for books, newspapers, songsheets, prayers, calendars, bulletins, teaching materials, etc., in short, wherever philological fine points are not in question and where reconversion to Hebrew is not called for.

Subsequently, Standards Committee Z-39 accepted the recommendation of the Subcommittee which includes the general-purpose system (and several other more complex systems for special purposes). On January 22, 1975, the ANSI Board of Standard Reviews approved the whole Standard as "The American National Standard Romanization of Hebrew" or ANSI Standard Z39.25. This Standard is available from the American National Standards Institute, 1430 Broadway, New York, New York 10018.

Dr. Werner Weinberg is Professor of Hebrew Language and Literature at the Hebrew Union College-Jewish Institute of Religion in Cincinnati; he serves as a member of the Subcommittee for the Romanization of Hebrew and Yiddish. Other members of the Subcommittee are: Mr. David L. Gold, Member, Committee for the Implementation of the Standardized Yiddish Orthography; Professor Lawrence Marwick, Head, Hebraic Section, Library of Congress; Dr. Menahem Schmelzer, Librarian, Jewish Theological Seminary of America; Professor Mordkhe Schaechter, Benyumen Shekhter Foundation for the

Advancement of Standard Yiddish; Mr. Allen B. Veaner, Assistant
Director for Bibliographic Operations, The Stanford University Li-
braries; and the undersigned, Chairman.

This booklet is Dr. Weinberg's work, not that of the Subcommittee;
but members of the Subcommittee read an early draft and made many
suggestions for which the author and the editor are grateful. More
than any other Subcommittee member, David L. Gold gave unsparingly
of his time and knowledge towards the development of the present
form of the booklet, and to him very special thanks are due.

A word of justification may be desirable in connection with the
inclusion of this work, not a bibliography, in the Bibliographica
Judaica series. For one thing, the title of the series implies bibliographical matters and not just bibliographies. For another,
since we feel that this general-purpose romanization is ideal for
the vast majority of books and other publications that are the
matter from which bibliography is made, it is entirely appropriate
that we address a book in the series to scholars generally, editors, authors, teachers and librarians and all who use romanization
in their writings.

The very considerable task of typing this book was graciously
undertaken by, and beautifully accomplished by Mrs. Gloria Wolfson.
The unusual problems of the design of the book were innovatively
solved by Noel Martin. To both of them my very warm thanks.

The reader now has a simple and authoritative Hebrew romanization system to follow; we hope it serves its purpose well.

-Herbert C. Zafren

To the Reader

It is proposed that the Romanization Table on the following pages serve as a standard for the conversion of Hebrew to Roman script for all general purposes in an English-speaking environment.

More questions and problems are connected with the romanization of Hebrew than meet the eye. They are dealt with in the body of this booklet.

By consulting the Table of Contents, the reader may select certain items that help him solve particular problems of romanization, he may want to read additional sections because they attract his interest, or he may decide to read the entire booklet in order to acquaint himself more fully with the question of romanization.

Even more useful than the Romanization Table, perhaps, may be the general and special word lists at the end. Here the reader may find, *already romanized*, a large number of the Hebrew words most commonly used in English. These lists, it is hoped, will reduce the chore of romanization at least until the reader becomes more familiar with the Table and how it is used.

Consonants

א	disregard; option: apostrophe at the beginning of a syllable within the word	מ ם	}	m
בּ	b	נ ן	}	n
ב	v	ס		s
גּ ג	} g	ע	same as א	
דּ ד	} d	פּ		p
ה	h	פ ף	}	f
ו	v	צ ץ	}	ts
ז	z	ק		k
ח	ch	ר		r
ט	t	שׁ		sh
י	y	שׂ		s
כּ ךּ	} k	תּ ת	}	t
כ ך	} ch			
ל	l			

Vowels

} a

} e

} e, é or ei*

(vocal) e or disregard*

} i

(kamats katan) } o

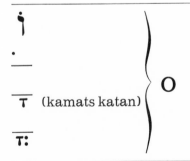
} u

depending on desired pronunciation

Special Situations

הָ -ah

הֶ -eh

הֵ -eh

הֹ -oh

יַ -ai

יָ -ai

יָו -av

הַ -h

makef	disregard
dagesh forte	disregard
prefixes	connect
capitalization	as one would in English
main stress*	by ʹ over vowel
syllabification*	by hyphen

if desired

Basic Terms and Assumptions

Romanization refers to rewriting in the Latin alphabet texts in a different script. It is a cover term for both *transliteration* and *transcription*, which in their narrow meanings signify a sign-for-sign and a sign-for-sound rendition, respectively.

In the Nelson Glueck Volume of the *Hebrew Union College Annual*, I published an article entitled "Transliteration and Transcription of Hebrew."[1] It is a detailed account accompanied by tables and charts. Readers of the present essay who are interested in the linguistic, historical and statistical aspects of the problem might want to consult it. For the purpose at hand, however, I need to cite only three principles developed in that article and proceed from there. The principles are:

(1) A single romanization of Hebrew for all purposes is neither practical nor desirable.

(2) Some types of romanizations lend themselves to international standardization.[2]

(3) Other types can be standardized only within a country or a community of countries that speak a given language and have a conventional way of writing it.

We are concerned here with the third category. The implication is that a general-purpose romanization should be "language-based," i.e., it should be standardized according to the way the sounds of a given language are rendered in its alphabet. For instance, the first sound of the word *shoe* is written *sh* in English, *sch* in German, *ch* in French and *sj* in Dutch. Members of these different language communities have every right to find Hebrew שׁ romanized in the form familiar to them rather than by the symbol *š* which serves the international community of scholars. Take another example: for Germans the letter *z* is the logical equivalent of Hebrew צ, but for Englishmen *z* is the equivalent of Hebrew ז. Due to the different sounds which letters of the Latin alphabet have come to represent in the different languages, there exist distinct English, German, or French spellings of Hebrew words which are used in these languages. Rather than deploring this fact, I propose that each language community should concentrate on standardizing its own spelling of Hebrew words. In doing so, it is unrealistic to expect the masses of readers of any language to bother with unfamiliar phonetic symbols and diacritics. For best results Hebrew must be rewritten in the alphabet characters to which readers are accustomed and which are phonetically meaningful to them. This principle may have the following implications: (1) when a Hebrew sound has no conventional rendition in the alphabet in question one must decide on a way of rendering it; (2) if one's own alphabet has several symbols for the same sound, only one of them must be selected to represent the sound in a Hebrew word; (3) if, inversely, a character of one's own alphabet can signify several sounds, only one of its phonetic renditions must be declared valid for a Hebrew word.

Some Specific Problems of English

We will henceforth deal with the English setting. Should any of the principles developed here prove to be of use for romanizations of Hebrew in other languages--so much the better!

Are there Hebrew sounds that are absent in the English language and, therefore, not represented in the English alphabet? There is really only one such sound, that of ח or כ. (We are not considering here the so-called Oriental pronunciation in which these two are distinguished.) In German this sound is written *ch*, in Dutch *g*, in Spanish *j*; but in English we must decide on a way of writing it. Hebrew צ has no single letter equivalent in English; but the sound does occur in English--e.g., in the word *pots* -- and it is best rendered *ts* (more below).

On the other hand, are there sounds which in English spelling are expressed in more than one way? As a matter of fact, all vowel sounds are. Let us take /u/ (ו or ‎ ֻ in Hebrew). It is written *u* in *sure, o* in *move, oe* in *shoe, oo* in *pool, ou* in *through, eu* and *oeu* in *maneuver* and *manoeuvre* respectively, *ui* in *fruit, ue* in *true, ieu* in *lieu* and *ew* in *Jew*. Similarly, /i/ (‎ ֵ or ‎ ֵ‎י in Hebrew) appears as *e* in *be*, as *ee* in *bee*, as *ei* in *seize*, as *ie* in *field*, as *ey* in *key*, as *eo* in *people*, as *ae* in *Caesar* and as *i* in machine. It is obvious that for the purpose of romanization a single choice of expressing each vowel must be made.

But not only is one vowel sound expressed in so many ways in English spelling--one written vowel sign can be read in several ways, e.g., the *a* in *father, fate, fat* and *fall*, or the *e* in *be, bed, bade, the* and *her*. Therefore the reader needs reading rules that tell him how to interpret the romanizer's intention correctly.

The need for reading instructions to accompany romanized Hebrew becomes even more obvious when we realize that we are by no means always sure about the reading of English words and that we do not mind receiving instructions from a writer or editor in the form of "*lead*--rhymes with *speed*," or the like. In the case of proper nouns the English writer and reader are often practically helpless. Almost habitually people (other than Smith and Jones and not too many others) spell their names out loud for the benefit of the listener and writer, and written names have a good chance of being mispronounced by the reader. When it comes to reading foreign names or words, many readers in the different languages will pronounce them to fit the phonetic values of their own alphabet. (Thus a German, unfamiliar with the name, may well pronounce every letter he sees in S-h-a-k-e-s-p-e-a-r-e, as the combinations *sh* and *ea* for one sound each as well as silent *e* are not found in German orthography.) This depends on an individual's education, but it is also a national characteristic of some peoples; it is especially so in the case of American readers. When *sputnik* made its first appearance in our press, the romanizer wanted to render the Russian *u* sound (he might have written *spootnik*); but it soon was pronounced like *spud* (rather than like *boot*). When they made fun of Germans pronouncing *Cincinnati Zinzinnati* they originally implied the pronunciation *Tsintsinati*, for in German *c* is pronounced *ts*, but that sound is usually rendered *z*. But due to American pronunciation based on spelling, the myth is now established that Germans say *Zinzinnati* with the English *z*--when nothing is further from the truth.

The Existing Hodgepodge

For all these reasons, Hebrew words used in English are written and, in turn, read in several ways. Thus we find the name of the peaceloving congregation spelled as *Ohev Shalom* or *Oheb* or *Ohef* or *Ohav* or *Sholom*; and the "Gates of Prayer" appear as *Shaarei Tefillah* or *Shaarey* or *Shaaray* or *Shaarai* or *Shaare* or *Share* or *Tefila* or *Tephilah* or *Tefilo*--one can list dozens of similar examples. And the *th* of *Beth, Adath, Agudath*--intended as a transliteration of Hebrew *tav* without *dagesh*, i.e., /t/--is read as the English *th* in *path*, the *J* of *Jeshurun* and the *z* in *Mizpah*--German transliterations for *yod* and *tsade* respectively--are read as the *J* in *Jew* and the *z* in *Liz*. Now these are examples from stable institutions, whose names are carved in stone on the House of God (*Beth-El, Bet El, Bethel*?); small wonder that we find a veritable hodgepodge in a romanized *Kadish*, on a Hebrew songsheet or in a Passover *Hagadah*. In the Jewish Religious Services column of the *New York Times* one may find the announcements of *Selichot, Selihot, Selichoth, Selihoth, Slichot, Slichos* or *Selichos* Services, or of the *Shevuoth, Shavuoth, Shabuoth, Shavuot, Shavuos, Shovuos* and *Shavuous* Festival.

The example of the word *Shaarei* above, showed five ways of rendering the Hebrew vowel *tsere*. Among favorite renditions of other vowels are *aw, ee, oo,* and *uh,* taken from English spelling values. The trend to use the unphonetic English spelling to render Hebrew phonetically culminates in the use of actual English words, as for instance: *oh-lay-new* or *beam-hay-raw*!

As for consonants, most romanization variants are found with regard to *chet* and *chaf* and to *tsade*. Certain scholarly transliterations sometimes spill over into popular usage, among them *ph* for *fe, th* for *tav* and *b* for *vet*. Other areas of diversity are: the rendering of *he* at the end of a word, the connecting of a prefix to the main word, and capitalization.

Is there then no fixed spelling, no standard for Hebrew words used in English? There is neither. One might expect to find a standard in Webster. The *Third New International Dictionary* contains hundreds of Hebrew words which are used in English, but what we find in Webster is "*hanukkah* or *hanukah* or *chanukah* also *chanukkah,* usu caps" and very many such options. A close study of Webster reveals certain *preferences*, e.g., *h* over *ch* and *tz* over *ts,* but they are not carried out consistently at all. Furthermore, Webster lists Sephardic, Ashkenazic, Yiddishized and plainly corrupt variants without indicating their different nature. In short, Webster only records existing spellings; the Dictionary does not set--nor does it attempt to set--a standard for romanized Hebrew.[3]

Earlier Attempts at Unification

Over the years a number of romanization systems for the English-speaking world have been developed. Notable among them are those of the *Jewish Encyclopedia* (1901), the British Royal Geographical Society (1921), the *Universal Jewish Encyclopedia* (1939), the Library of Congress (1948), the U. S. Board on Geographical Names

(1961) and the *Encyclopaedia Britannica* (revised 1964).[4] To these may be added systems used by the different journals in the areas of Judaica and Hebraica.

But all these systems were designed for more or less philological purposes, as Hebrew spelling features play a role in them (if not consistently so), e.g., differentiating between *tet* and *tav* or *kaf* and *kuf* or the doubling of a letter for *dagesh*. The rendition of such features has no conceivable function in a general-purpose romanization, but it is necessary for *special* purposes. I, too, advocate a more exact romanization (see below page 32) although not before proposing a popular or general-purpose romanization which can serve in English-speaking countries on perhaps ninety per cent of all occasions when romanized Hebrew is needed, and for which no proposal for unity and a standard has so far come forth.

Standardization Can Be Achieved

I can only guess why a proposal of this kind has not been made. One reason may well be the feeling that it is a hopeless undertaking to try to bring order into the existing chaos and that, even if romanizers agree on a system, their public will not read the romanization correctly. Another reason might be a certain arrogance on the part of scholars that has kept them from designing a popular romanization, even though the users of a general-purpose romanization may be counted in the hundreds of thousands. Finally, I can imagine that the idea of having different "national" romanizations seems to stand in direct contrast to the idea of unity.

If these indeed be the reasons for the absence of a serious unification proposal, I would counter them by saying: It is easier to achieve a standard for a language-centered ("national") general-purpose romanization than for any other type (like a more exact or a strictly scientific one) because the field is not strewn with proposals, because the users of such a system are not hampered by scholarly scruples concerning this or that detail, but most of all because there exists a great demand, a real public need for unification in this area.

The Gordian knot of the inability of the masses to read romanized Hebrew correctly can be severed by means of a short, simple pronunciation guide.

Recognizing *de jure* an English, French, German, etc., romaniza-

tion of Hebrew and setting a standard for each--far from furthering disunity--eliminates the multiple ways now existing within the
different language communities. As to the implementation of a proposed standard, it is of great importance that it be endorsed and
furthered by an authoritative body in the different countries. In
the United States such a body is the American National Standard Institute.

Uses and Users

Some areas of use for the general-purpose romanization are: bulletins, posters, programs, announcements and communications by congregations and other Jewish organizations or institutions; romanized sections in prayer books, hymnals and Passover *Hagadot*; writing on the blackboard, mimeographed services or presentations,
songsheets, summer camp materials; Hebrew lessons and vocabularies;
maps of Israel; catalogue cards of synagogue, school or center lib-
raries; Jewish calendars;[5] Jewish newspapers and periodicals; text-
books and other books of Jewish content including Bible translations; but also general books and publications that contain Hebrew
words; furthermore encyclopedias, dictionaries, yearbooks and other
works of reference. These areas point at the following persons who
would romanize Hebrew in the course of their work: rabbis and all
Jewish functionaries; faculty or staff or students of Jewish institutions of learning, of congregations, of national or local organizations, of community centers, camps, agencies and homes; furthermore volunteer workers, writers, editors, printers and publishers. All these--and perhaps publishers in particular--could help
to achieve unity in the romanization of Hebrew by adopting a standard and adhering to it.

A special word is in order for both Jewish and non-Jewish scholars. There are occasions when they need a more exact or even a
very exact romanization; however, for the majority of their work
the general-purpose style would be quite sufficient. The great
effort by author, editor, printer and proofreader that goes into a
sophisticated transliteration is largely unwarranted. There seem
to be three reasons why a scholar would insist on delivering his
complicated (and expensive) romanization: tradition, fear of being
misunderstood, and prestige. These can be countered as follows:
(1) Which or whose tradition: For there has never been a single,

generally accepted system of scientific transliteration. (2) He should credit his fellow scholars with enough intelligence to recognize his intention even from a simple romanization. (3) A scientific transliteration is a mechanical skill; it does not prove a person's scholarship. The scholar does not impress his colleagues by it. However, they may well frown at his using the general-purpose romanization. On the other hand, they just might appreciate his courage in breaking a taboo, and many may follow his example. Incidentally, there is nothing agaist "mixing" romanization styles; i.e., the scholar can render Hebrew words in the general-purpose style; but when it comes to demonstrating a philological point, he may write the word in a narrow transliteration or any other style the situation calls for (cf. footnote 2).

Some Principles of a General-Purpose Romanization

(Readers who might wish to forego all theory and to accept the system as proposed in the Romanization Table are advised to turn to the annotated samples, pages 36-43 and the word lists, pages 43-57.)

(1) The system must be simple; it must contain nothing but alphabet characters all of which are found on the typewriter.

(2) The system is basically a phonetic transcription in that it renders identical sounds (homophones) by one sign, even when Hebrew has more than one for them; e.g., ח and כ.

(3) A person who wants to romanize according to rules or a standard must be able to *read* pointed Hebrew; he does not need to *understand* the language.

(4) The proposed romanization aims at the general Israeli pronunciation (this name is preferable to *Sephardic*; the two are really not the same).[6] The "Oriental" pronunciation of *chet* and *ayin* used by some Israeli speakers and promoted by a number of educators is not considered. However, since Ashkenazic is also used in English-speaking countries, a special section will be devoted to it (below, page 31).

(5) Proper nouns--family and given names, names of congregations, organizations, businesses, etc.--are not covered by the rules, if there exists an accepted or a traditional spelling, e.g., *Aschkenazy, Hayim* or *Ḥayyim* or *Chaim, Bene Zedek, B'nai B'rith.* On the other hand, individuals or organizations may want to change the spelling of such a name to comply with the proposed standard.[7]

(6) The romanizer needs more than a conversion table of consonants and vowels. His guide must include a number of "special situations," as for instance instructions whether or not to double a
letter for the strong *dagesh,* whether to hyphenate pref[i]xes, when
to capitalize and so forth.

(7) In this booklet, cited Hebrew forms appear in italics so as
to make them stand out. However, in most general-purpose situations
this is not necessary.

(8) Without an accepted standard, a romanizer may write a Hebrew word, hopeful or perhaps even convinced that he has rendered
it in such a way that his reader will pronounce it correctly. But
the reader's mind does not necessarily function like the writer's
mind. A working understanding between the two can only be achieved
by setting down writing rules for the writer and reading rules for
the reader. It is very important that a romanizer not accept a
standard "with small changes" or "with slight adjustments." A standard must be accepted in its entirety; otherwise the chaos begins
anew. There are, and ought to be, a number of options, as will be
shown below, but these are variants within the standard.

Detailed Considerations

The following sections strive to make the subject more lucid,
not more complicated. They are written for the benefit of readers
who like to be a party to the reasoning behind the rules, and they
try to anticipate problems beyond mere transposing of letters
which the romanizer will face, and to offer guidance toward solving
them.

Homophones

No less than twelve Hebrew alphabet letters form pairs of homophones: א and ע, ב and ו, ח and כ, ט and ת, כ and ק, ס and שׂ. By
disregarding mere orthographic differences, we may occasionally
come up with an ambiguity in our romanization. For instance, by
writing *Kol Yisrael* we leave the reader guessing whether קוֹל or
-כָּל is meant, but such cases are not very frequent.

Alef and *Ayin*

Among the pairs of homophones, *alef* and *ayin* are in a special
category because we are used to characterizing them as "soundless,"

and this is indeed correct for most practical purposes. For a general-purpose romanization it is of no consequence that the words *El* and *Al* are spelled with an *alef* and an *ayin* respectively; neither one is phonetically meaningful. But within a word, the presence of *alef* and *ayin* can make a difference by audibly indicating the onset of a syllable, thus for instance in both words of *Tish'ah Be'av*. Really it is not so much the letters *alef* and *ayin* the romanizer is interested in rendering with his apostrophe (it should be the *straight* apostrophe, also in print), but the syllable-dividing effect *alef* and *ayin* have in these positions in carefully enunciated Hebrew speech.

The cases of *Tish'ah* and *Be'av* are somewhat different in kind. Not because one word is spelled with *ayin* and the other with *alef*-- this difference plays no role whatsoever in a general-purpose romanization. Rather the difference lies in the fact that in the first word the syllabic boundary occurs between a consonant and a vowel (postconsonantal *alef* and *ayin*) and in the second, between two vowels (intervocalic *alef* and *ayin*). In the first situation speakers (including Israelis) are inclined to ignore the boundary, syllabifying *Ti-shah* rather than *Tish-ah*. If a romanizer is interested in achieving the precise enunciation he will put an apostrophe in the place of postconsonantal *alef* or *ayin*, e.g., *lir'ot, shiv'ah, tif'eret, hif'il, chir'uteh, tum'ah, mal'ach*. If, for the purpose of a song sheet or a prayer, the romanizer syllabifies every word by means of hyphens, it is of course not necessary to write the apostrophe as well; for instance, *ve-ha-tif-e-ret* (not: *ve-ha-tif-'e-ret*).

In the case of an intervocalic *alef* or *ayin* (*Be'av*) the apostrophe fulfills an additional task. By indicating the syllabic boundary it prevents the two vowels (here *ea*) from being read as one in the English way (as in *beaver* or *bear*). While the romanizer does not want to clutter up the word with unnecessary apostrophes, he must, on the other hand, prevent a misreading of this type. True, one of the Reading Rules (below, page 31) tells the reader to separate two vowels (except when they stand for diphthongs), but the romanizer may want to employ an extra apostrophe to offset English reading habits.

In English there are some vowel combinations which are not normally or usually read as a single vowel; e.g., *aa, ao, ia, ii, io, iu, ua, uo, uu.* Consequently, when these combinations occur in Hebrew words, they can be more or less safely written without an intervening apostrophe; e.g., *Haarets, Maoz, Tekiah, Neviim, Yediot, shiur, pual, Shavuot.*

With other combined vowels the English reading value can be either one or two vowels. The criterion for the reader in making his decision is whether or not he knows or recognizes the word in English. He is not likely to misinterpret the vowels in *Laertes* and *Caesar, naive* and *nail, real* and *reach, nuclear* and *clear, reelect* and *reel, deity* and *seize, deign, reorganize* and *people, Leo* and *Leonard, Daniel* and *shlemiel, diet* and *died, retroactive* and *oak, doeth* and *does, goeth* and *goes, coincide* and *coin, zoology* and *zoo, suet* and *sued, fruition* and *fruit.* When such vowel combinations occur in Hebrew words the romanizer must use his judgment with regard to the apostrophe. He may even "try out" a word on paper with and without an apostrophe, seeking to predict whether or not his readers are liable to mispronounce it.[8]

Other English vowel clusters generally stand for a single sound or a diphthong, e.g., *au, eu, ou, oi.* If an *alef* or *ayin* occurs between these vowels, the romanizer may prefer to use the apostrophe as a reminder to the reader to separate them, e.g., *haatsma'ut, se'udah, bo'u, mo'il.* What is true for *oi* is also valid for the combinations *ai, ei* and *ui* when they do *not* stand for a diphthong in Hebrew, e.g., *tsa'ir, she'im, kru'im.*

Special care must be taken when the Hebrew word without an apostrophe happens to look like an English word, e.g., *meat (me'at), reach (re'ach), veal (ve'al), beer (be'er), hair (ha'ir), Mr. Neeman (Ne'eman).*

In cases of "furtive *patach*" like לְשַׁבֵּחַ or גִּלְבֹּעַ, the vowels may be separated by an apostrophe even though it does not stand for an *alef* or *ayin,* thus *leshabe'ach, Gilbo'a.*

ch versus *kh, ḥ* and *h*

The sound of *chet* or *chaf* has variously been presented in English romanizations as *h, ḥ, kh* and *ch.* These four ways of writing can be characterized as follows: *h* is the closest English phonetic substitute for the Hebrew sound; *ḥ* and *kh* are the symbols used in scholarly transliterations, the first for *chet,* the other for *chaf; ch* finally is the normal German transcription of the sound. English took it over together with other German romanizations, as German Hebraic scholarship and German Jewish emigration spread to English-speaking countries.

English itself has the sound as well as the *ch*-writing, at least in theory, in the often cited Scottish word *loch* and, on a practical level, in the exclamation *yech*! (variations: *eech, ooch, wooch*) or the word *eechy*.

Of the four renditions listed above, *h* must be ruled out; it should stand only for Hebrew ה. (If we write *Hanukah*, how can the reader differentiate the first letter from the one in *Hagadah*?) On the other hand, *ḥ* and *kh* make sense only if one wants to differentiate between *chet* and *chaf*, which is not the case in a general-purpose romanization. (To use either *ḥ* or *kh* for both *chet* and *chaf* runs counter to the tradition of scholarly transliteration; it is bound to create problems.) This leaves *ch*, which is in fact well entrenched in the English romanization of Hebrew. It is the only one of the German loan romanizations which should remain.

ts versus *tz*

Writing *tz* for Hebrew צ is another vestige of German romanization and is likewise entrenched in some cases (*Bar Mitzvah, matzah, chalutz*, etc.). But the situation is different from that of *ch*. Both the sound of Hebrew צ and a way of writing it exist in English; e.g., *lots, rabbits, Betsy*. In *tsetse fly* it is also found at the beginning of a word. It makes no difference that the writing consists of two letters and the sound is felt to be a composite--it corresponds exactly to צ, better than *tz*--the second part of which is not contained in the Hebrew sound at all, and which fits German but not English alphabet values. The same is true for *z* (without the *t*) so that the writing *Zahal* (the Israeli army) will be read correctly by the German but not by the English reader. For the latter, *ts* is the best rendition of צ. Yet when a romanizer is very hesitant about writing words like *Bar Mitzvah*, etc. with *ts*, he may treat them as *exceptions* in which the conventionalized *tz* may be used instead of the preferable *ts*.

Digraphs

The letter combinations *ch* and *ts* are called digraphs--two letters expressing one sound. A third digraph is *sh* for שׁ. An argu-

ment against the use of digraphs in romanizations is that the
reader might take them for separate signs, reading *mac-hon* instead
of *ma-chon*, *Bit-saron* instead of *Bi-tsaron*, *mos-hav* instead of
mo-shav. However, this source of error is small, and it exists,
inversely, in English itself--where one might read digraphs i.e.
one sound in words like *nuthatch*, *mishap*, *haphazard* and the like.
The group *th* is an English digraph, not a Hebrew one. If it occurs
in a romanized word the two sounds must be pronounced separately,
as stated in the Reading Rules (below, page 31). The romanizer may
go an extra step by placing an apostrophe between the letters,
e.g., *veyit'hadar*. (He may do the same when *sh* is to be separated,
e.g., in Ashkenazic *veyis'hadar*.) The digraph *ph* for /f/ occurs in
established spellings like *Ephraim*.

a, e, i, o, u

These five vowels suffice to render the Hebrew vocalization even
though the traditional system has no less than seventeen vowel
points and vowel point combinations (see vowel column in the Romanization Table). Whatever the nuances once were--for instance, between ⸱, ⸱ and ⸱ --they have now disappeared. It is true that *ee*
and *aw* would be phonetically meaningful and unambiguous for the
English reader (*oo* is not unambiguous; see *food* and *flood*). Furthermore, combinations with *h*--*ah*, *eh*, *uh*--are common and render
definite vowel values. However, *a*, *e*, *i*, *o*, *u*, are probably the
only vowel notations on which it will be possible to achieve agree-
ment. Admittedly, English will need reading rules for all of them
(unlike German, Italian, Spanish, etc.), but this is the price that
must be paid for unity.

ei (or Perhaps *é*) for *Tsere*

The Romanization Table gives an option of rendering *tsere* by *ei*
instead of *e*, "depending on the pronunciation intended." This
refers to the diphthongal pronunciation, an Ashkenazic feature
which can also sometimes be observed in Israeli speech.

In English words this diphthong is rendered *ei*, e.g., in *freight*;
but it appears also as *ey* (in *they*), as *ay* (in *May*), as *ai* (in
maid) or as simple *a* (in *made*). Why is *ei* chosen of all these? Because the *y* in *ay* and *ey* must be saved for the consonant (as in
Beyisrael and *bayit*), the *ai* combination for the diphthong in וַיְ

(more below), and *a* of course, serves for the simple (monophthongal) vowel.

It is especially the stressed *tsere* at the end of the word, which the romanizer may want to write *ei*, e.g., *Mishlei, yehei, shmeih* (i.e., ֵי , ֵא and Aramaic ֵה). He also may want to employ *ei* when simple *e* results in a word that is identical with an English one, e.g., *he, male, shave, chaser*. But usually, simple *e* is sufficient, especially since a reading rule calls attention to this *e* at the end of the word (below page 31).

He may also place an acute accent on *e*, (indicating a tense, monophthongal pronunciation of *tsere*) e.g., *Mishlé, hé, chasér* He has the same liberty here as with English words like *résumé, cliché* or *élite*.

Indicating the *Shva*

The *shva* sound has often been rendered by an apostrophe. However, nowhere in English does the apostrophe stand for the *shva* sound; cf. *don't, you're, Joe's, boys'*. Besides, in the proposed system the apostrophe is preempted as a syllable divider indicating *alef* and *ayin* (above, page 20).

It is best to express the *shva* , too, by *e*. This vowel sign is thus used for a number of vocalic variants, e.g. in *beseder* (offhand one cannot know whether the second *e* in *levavecha* is a *shva* or a stressed *segol*, whether the *e* in *beni* is a *shva* or a *tsere*). But the same ambiguity is present in English *preferred* or German *gegeben*. It only illustrates the fact that normal writing is limited in rendering phonetic detail. One must often know a word or learn it before one can read it correctly.

A more pertinent question is when to indicate the *shva* and when not, e.g., *kneset* or *keneset, shma* or *shema, brit* or *berit, shomré* or *shomeré, veshamru* or *veshameru, uvchol* or *uvechol, kidshanu* or *kideshanu, hadvarim* or *hadevarim, ve'imru* or *ve'imeru, vayhi (vay-hi)* or *vayehi, hamvorach* or *hamevorach*? The pointed text does not help because the vocal *shva* and the silent one look alike. The direction given in the Romanization Table "depending on the desired pronunciation" does not seem to be very helpful either, yet it sums up the reality of handling the *shva* in a general-purpose romanization.

Definite rules about the *shva* are found in all Hebrew grammar books. They have come to us from the sixteenth century and stipu-late five cases in which a *shva* is vocal, all others being silent.[9] The trouble with these rules is threefold: (1) They are both com-plicated and vague, and the average romanizer cannot be expected to handle them. (2) Many grammarians cast doubt on the scientific soundness of some of the rules. (3) The grammatically vocal *shvas* are pronounced nowadays only by expert Torah readers; they are dis-regarded in much of liturgical Hebrew and most of spoken Hebrew.

No new rules have emerged that would cover the use of *shva* in spoken Hebrew. It appears as a "free" vowel which sometimes is pronounced and sometimes omitted. (Interestingly, it was often used in the same way in medieval poetry to accommodate the syllable count.) Where does this leave the romanizer?

Let us assume he knows Hebrew grammar well and recognizes each grammatically vocal *shva*--he may still be wrong in rendering it because it is not really pronounced . (In a purely scholarly transliteration all these *shvas* would indeed be rendered.) Prac-tically speaking, a romanizer must go by the way he has *heard* the Hebrew word in speech, recitation, chant or song and wants it re-produced. If he knows Hebrew well, he may occasionally be correc-tive, inserting a *shva* where he heard none or omitting it where one is pronounced. If, on the other hand, a romanizer does not know the sound of words at all (knowing only how to decipher Hebrew script), his rendition of *shvas* will be erratic. However, this will not impede the rest of his romanization too seriously. Some guidance may be found in the annotated samples, pages 36-43.

The Endings -*ah, -eh* and -*oh* versus -*a, -e* and -*o*

In English there exists a general preference to render the end-ing הָ -*ah*, e.g., *menorah*. By analogy the endings הֶ or הֵ and הֹ- should be rendered -*eh* and -*oh* respectively. However, since many romanizers omit the *h*, it is better to make its writing optional, thus *menorah* or *menora, mikveh* or *mikve, Shlomoh* or *Shlomo*. Roman-izers may divide the option, rendering הָ -*a*, because, in English words, -*a* at the end is sounded (e.g., *Alabama*), but romanizing הֶ- -*eh* because -*e* at the end of English words is usually silent. The ending הֹ- is rare. Romanizers may want to render it -*oh* in order to distinguish it from the ending וֹ-.

Hebrew words ending with ָ, יֵ and וֹ- (בֵיתוֹ, בָּתֵּי, בֵיתָהּ) should

25

not be romanized with -h, thus, *betcha*, *bate*, *beto* even though
phonetically there is no difference between these and words ending with ה. The same is true of words ending in *alef*, e.g., *Gemara*,
rofe (גמרָא, רוֹפֵא) or with *ayin* e.g., *Shma*, *shome'a* (שְׁמַע, שׁוֹמֵעַ).
The *h* in the following pairs must therefore be considered a con-
cession to orthographic (as opposed to phonetic) writing: *Chevrah*
and *Kadisha* (חֶבְרָה קַדִישָׁא), *veyitnase* and *veyitaleh* (וִיתְנַשֵּׂא
וְיִתְעַלֶּה), *poh* and *bo* (פֹּה בֹּו or בּוֹא).

ai (also oi and ui)

The י in the ending ־י is really consonantal (for instance in
יָדַי). If we wanted to be corrective here too, we might prefer *ay*.
But ־י is always pronounced like a diphthong, and parallel to
writing the *tsere* diphthong with an *i*, namely, *ei*, we must render
this diphthong *ai*. Furthermore, the writing *ay* would be in contrast to established spellings as in *Hagai*, *Adonai*, *Sinai*, *Mordecai*.
There is little chance that *ai* will be pronounced as in *wait* because we are used to pronouncing it correctly in foreign words, for
instance in *Thailand*, *Hawaii*, *Saigon*.

If in a different form the י of ־י has a vowel and consequently
becomes audibly consonantal, it is written *y*, like every consonantal י. Thus *yadai* but *yadayim*. If the י has a *shva* (as in הַבַּיְתָה or
לַיְלָה) the romanizer must decide between a diphthongal or a consonantal rendition by writing *lailah* or *laylah*, *habaitah* or *habaytah*.
This depends on how he hears it and how he wants it to be pronounced.

Corresponding with *ei* and *ai*, the other diphthongs are written
oi and *ui*. Here too, the י is rendered by *y* when it becomes consonantal, e.g., *goi-goyim*, *ilui-iluyim*.

If successive *e* and *i*, *a* and *i*, *o* and *i*, or *u* and *i* are to render the individual vowels they indicate rather than diphthongs,
the romanizer is well-advised to separate them by an apostrophe
(above, page 21).

No Need for Doubling Letters

In scholarly transliteration a letter containing a strong *dagesh*
is doubled. Also, in popular use words like *Hallel*, *Kaddish*,
kibbuts, *Kiddush*, *Kippur*, *Shabbat*, *siddur*, *shidduch*, *sukkah*, *Sukkot*.
Tammuz, *Haggadah*, *Kabbalah*, *Megillah*, *Tefillin*, are probably more

frequently spelled with a double consonant than with a single one.
This letter-doubling may be a vestige of the doubling for the
strong *dagesh*; it also agrees with English spelling habits. However,
neither reason is valid: in modern Hebrew the strong *dagesh* has no
doubling force; in fact, it has no influence on the pronunciation
at all.[10] And as to consonant-doubling after a short vowel in Eng-
lish--this occurs irregularly. We have *inn*, but also *in*; *add*, but
also *ad*. Words like *rapid, leper, primer, oven* or *study* have a single consonant after a short vowel. The doubling of the consonant in
Hebrew words like those listed above also has the disadvantage of
furthering the incorrect (in Israeli pronunciation) penultimate
stress, e.g., *Shábbat, Súkkot*; in fact, this Ashkenazic stress may
well have contributed to the consonant doubling in popular romanization. Finally, consistent doubling for *dagesh* would entail doubling of the digraphs *sh* and *ts*, as well as doubling of the letter
following the article and other prefixes, e.g., *Kedushshah, matstsah,
Hattikvah*. For all these reasons it is better not to double at all.

The doubling of *s* is a special case, since present habits will
apply it occasionally also when the preceding vowel is not short
and the Hebrew word does not have a *dagesh* in the ס or שׁ, e.g.,
Knesset or *chassid*. This may--once again--be a German romanization,
since in German single *s* stands for the voiced *s* (as in *easy*),
while unvoiced *s* (as in *mason*) is written in German either with a
special character or otherwise with double *s*. In English the writing *s* or *ss* is not necessarily related to the length of the preceding vowel (the vowels are of equal length in *grass* and *gas*, *miss*
or *mis-*) and, to begin with, an *s* is read unvoiced rather than
voiced, especially in unknown words. Therefer, *Kneset* would normally be pronounced with the correct *s*-sound, and doubling of *s* is
unnecessary in the romanization of Hebrew words.

And yet--as in the case of *ts* over *tz* (above, page 22)--when all
is said and done, some romanizers will prefer the conventionalized
spelling with double consonants in words like those quoted above.
If they do so, they should look upon them as *exceptions* to the preferable spelling with one consonant.

No Reason to Hyphenate Prefixes to the Word

The habit of hyphenating prefixes--*ha-bayit, la-bayit, mi-bayit*
--is founded on the idea that we are really dealing here with more

than one word and that the main word should stand out clearly. This habit must be discouraged for several reasons. First of all, the concept of what exactly constitutes a word is not always absolutely clear even in English, and one should certainly not apply English concepts to other languages. In Hebrew these prefixes are written as part of the word, and we are only romanizing Hebrew words, not interpreting them (if we feel that *habayit* 'the house' is "really" two words, is *babayit* 'in the house' perhaps "really" three?). Secondly, it was said above (page 18) that a romanizer requires only a reading knowledge of Hebrew, not an understanding of the language. But using the hyphen for separating prefixes requires such knowledge, for words may begin with *ha-*, *ba-*, *mi-*, etc., which are *not* prefixes, but part of the main word, e.g., in *hatslachah*, *bakashah*, *mishloach*.

Capitalization

One might argue that since Hebrew has no capital letters a romanization must not have them either. While this conclusion would be true for a strictly scientific transliteration, it does not hold for our general-purpose romanization. The latter follows English writing habits, and capitalization is one of them. The directive in the Romanization Table "as one would in English" needs elaboration; especially since capitalization in English is not always a mechanical matter.[11]

(1) The following categories of words must always be capitalized:[12] proper nouns; geographical names; names of organizations, institutions and movements; the beginning of a sentence or a line of poetry, of a song or a prayer; the title or heading of a book or an article; holidays, festivals and religious seasons; the Jewish months; prayers which have a distinct name and fixed prayer times or Services; Torah Portions and Talmud or Mishnah or Tosefta Tractates or Chapters (*Perakim*).

(2) In the case of other words for Jewish customs and ceremonies, ceremonial objects, religious functionaries, etc., context and intention must determine capitalization. The Word List (below page 46) can be of some guidance; but the decision often rests with the romanizer. The mere fact that a word is Hebrew should not warrant its capitalization.[13] Words that appear in lower case in the Word List must be capitalized at the beginning of a sentence or a

line of poetry, etc., but certain circumstances may warrant their capitalization in the middle of a sentence, too. Words that appear in the list in both lower and upper case (e.g., *baal* or *Baal*, *chumash* or *Chumash*), have a slightly different meaning in each writing. Words, finally, that are listed only with a capital letter belong to one of the categories listed under (1), which are always to be capitalized. But even here the romanizer may disagree. If for instance, *Birkat Hamazon* is capitalized since it is a "prayer with a distinct name," he may want to write it lower case because in his context he would write also *grace after meals*. For those nuances of meaning that cause a person to write either *confirmation* or *Confirmation*, *weekly portion* or *Weekly Portion*, *eternal light* or *Eternal Light* the directive "as one would in English" makes good sense. For some, Webster's definition may be helpful, namely, one capitalizes "because of the particularizing or individualizing significance of capitals as against the generic or generalizing significance of lower case" (*The New International Dictionary*, page 29a). The following are some examples of applying this principle: "Mr. Cohen is a *chazan*," but "*Chazan* Cohen"; "he attended a *yeshivah*," but "he attended the Volozhin *Yeshivah*"; "a *halachah*" (a law), but "the *Halachah*" (the legal system); "the word for *president* is *nasi*," but "*Nesi Yisrael*" or "*Yehudah Hanasi*"; "this is a *minhag*," but "*Minhag Ashkenaz*"; "the exam contained one *mishnah* and one *midrash*," but "they study *Mishnah* and *Midrash*"; "the Five *Megilot* are found in the Bible part *Ketuvim*," but "they found five *megilot* near the Dead Sea"; "this month three *bar mitsvahs* took place," but "the *Bar Mitsvah* of . . . will take place on . . ." All this not withstanding, capitalization will often be a matter of feeling and personal interpretation.

(3) When capitals are used for terms that consist of several words, capitalize all of them, e.g., *Meah She'arim*, *Histradrut Haovdim*, *Kiryat Shmonah*, *Shivah Asar Betamuz*. In a term like *Yom Sheni Shel Sukot*, a grammarian might argue that *shel* is a syntactical link rather than part of the name; yet he will have to admit that it cannot be omitted from the name and is, therefore, part of it. A romanizer who knows enough Hebrew to identify a term that must be capitalized will in most cases be able to say which words belong to that term.

(4) In the case of a word with a prefix it is the prevailing use

to capitalize the latter, e.g., *Rosh Hashanah, Lag Baomer, Achad Haam* and not *haShanah, baOmer* or *haAm*. So also: *Hamotsi, Hatorah, Torah Vaavodah, Vedavid, Ushlomoh, Betamuz, Leyisrael, Kemosheh, Lishmuel, Mitel-Aviv, Me'erets Mitsrayim, Birushalayim, Vihudah.* While this mode of writing may seem illogical (it is the main word that needs capitalization and not the prefix) it is less objection- able than having a capital letter in the middle of a word. By writ- ing a word-to-be capitalized together with its prefix, as Hebrew orthography requires, we really have little choice but to capitalize the romanized word at its beginning, if we want it to look natu- ral.[14] Perhaps if words are syllabified (e.g., for a song sheet), the word proper can be capitalized, e.g., *be-Yis-ra-el, ke-Mosheh,* due to the visible separation of the prefix. But this exception does not stand up in cases like *Bi-ru-sha-la-yim, La-do-nai* or *Ke-lo-he-nu,* where the prefix and the beginning of the main word are fused into one syllable.

Will Options and Exceptions not Further Disunity?

In the course of these explanations the romanizer has been given options in five cases: (1) expressing *alef* or *ayin* within a word or disregarding it; (2) rendering *tsere* as *e, ei* or *é*; (3) rendering *shva* or disregarding it; (4) rendering the endings ﬦָ, ﬦֶ, ﬦֱ and ﬦ- either with or without *h*; (5) rendering the group ﬦַ as *ai* or *ay*. Furthermore two exceptions have been stated: (1) *tz* instead of *ts* and (2) double instead of single consonant in case the romanizer prefers conventionalized, over standard, spelling of certain words.

The question may be asked why options are given and exceptions allowed when a new system is to be introduced. Will they not open the door to arbitrariness when the very purpose of the system is unification? But it is rather absolute decisiveness and rigidity, in cases which by their nature allow for more than one possibility, that encourage deviation and with it breakdown of the system. Romanization must not be stricter than national orthographies and these allow for options and exceptions. Users of the proposed sys- tem who desire further guidance are referred to the Annotated Sam- ples (pages 36-43) and the Word Lists (pages 43-57), where prefer- ences are expressed.

Reading Rules

If somebody is a fluent Hebrew-reader, the romanization will
readily call to mind the original Hebrew and he will read correctly.
But somebody who reads Hebrew poorly or not at all needs assistance
in interpreting the romanization correctly. A pronunciation guide
like the Reading Rules below should accompany every large body of
romanized material; and users, like a synagogue choir, summer camp-
ers or an adult study group, should be repeatedly exposed to it. In
addition to learning the rules they should be given oral instructions and drills.

Vowels

a   as in *papa* (short) or *father* (long). Not as in *ale, care, add*
     or *all*.

e   as in *get* (short), *cafe* (long) or *the (shva)*. Not as in *equal*
     or *pretty*.

e   at the end of a word is stressed as in *cafe* and not silent as
     in *safe*.

i   as in *bit* (short) or *machine* (long). Not as in *bite*.

o   as in *often* (short). Not as in *job* nor in *Job*.

u   as in *pull* (short) or *rule* (long). Not as in *but* or *use*.

ai   as in *aisle*. Not as in *wait*.

ei   as in *veil*. Not as in *height* or *ceiling*.

Except for diphthongs *ai, ei, oi* and *ui* always separate between two
successive vowels.

Consonants

ch   as in Scottish *loch* or German *ach*. Not as in *chart, character*
     or *charade*.

g   as in *get*. Not as in *gem*.

th   as in *nuthatch* (two different sounds).

Ashkenazic Hebrew[15]

A conversion of the Romanization Table to the Ashkenazic pronunciation requires the following: ת and ת must be distinguished;
the former is romanized *t*, the latter *s*. ָ is *o* (as in *border*)
rather than *a* and consequently the endings הָ and יָ are -*oh* (or
-*o*) and -*ov* respectively. The *cholam* (both ֹ and ו) is likewise
rendered *o*, the same as in Israeli pronunciation; but it is read

31

diphthongal (as in *bold*). Thus in *sholom* the first *o* is simple (monophthongal), the second diphthongal. If a romanizer wants to bring out the difference he has the option to render the *cholam ou*, thus *sholoum*. The two words *shabas sholoum* contain all the important differences between Ashkenazic and Israeli pronunciation *shabat shalom*. If the romanizer renders the Ashkenazic *cholam ou*, the reading rule is: "as in *soul*; not as in *sound* or in *souvenir*." The Ashkenazic romanizer usually prefers *ei* over *e* for *tsere*. See the Ashkenazic text sample, page 38.

A More Exact System

For a limited number of purposes romanizers may want to apply a system that has a closer relationship to Hebrew orthography without going to the extreme of a really exact sign-by-sign transliteration. Among such purposes may be catalogue cards in a specialized or research library, scientific encyclopedias, dictionaries, gazeteers or maps of Israel and Hebrew words in a philological context. Romanizers not interested in these categories may as well omit reading this section.

The more exact romanization is distinguished from the general-purpose one mainly by the distinct rendition of the consonant homophones, viz.:

א and ע = ' and ' (curved apostrophe and its reverse)

ב and ו = v and w

ח and כ = ḥ and kh

ט and ת = ṭ and t

כ and ק = k and q

ס and שׂ = s and ś

The characters for *alef* and *ayin* as well as *ḥ*, *ṭ* and *ś* use diacritics. They, together with the others on this list, are widely accepted for differentiating between the Hebrew homophones.

It is well to call the reader's attention to the fact that *w* for ו only signifies an orthographic differentiation and does not refer to the English sound of the letter.

In the more exact system *ayin* is always rendered, while *alef* is omitted at the beginning of a word.

In print, the symbols for *alef* and *ayin* are the curved apostrophe and its reverse (they may also be described as a raised comma and its reverse). They can also be rendered as small, raised semi-

circles open to the left and the right respectively. On the typewriter it is best to skip a space and fill the symbol in by hand
(do not use the straight apostrophe in the more exact system). Some
romanizers working with the typewriter render *alef* as a question
mark and *ayin* by a raised letter *c* (because their curvatures resem-
ble the shapes of the apostrophe and its reverse.)

The romanizer has the option of doubling a letter for the strong
dagesh or not, but he would not double a digraph (*matsah*, not
matstsah; *Kedushah*, not *Kedushshah*) or any letter after a prefix
(*Hatikvah*, not *Hattikvah*). The diphthongs יַ, וֹי and וּי are rendered *ay*, *oy*, *uy* rather than *ai*, *oi*, *ui*, because in the more exact
system we want to insist on the consonantal character of the *yod*
(in יֶ and יִ and the ending יו‎ָ it is not consonantal).

The vowels of the more exact system remain the same five basic
ones as in the general-purpose system. Any differentiation here not
only opens the vista of having to account for all those seventeen
Masoretic vowel notations but also confronts the romanizer with the
fact that there exists no generally accepted system or standard for
their romanization.

Except for the pointing, the more exact system is "reversible,"
i.e., the romanization could be mechanically reverted to the Hebrew
alphabet. In order to maintain this quality, consistency is recommended in differentiating between all six pairs of homophones. One
must not be selective about this (for instance,differentiating between ח and כ, but not between ט and ת), as many romanizers do.

Foreign and International Words

(1) When a proper noun transcribed from a language using the
Roman alphabet is found in Hebrew, a romanizer may want to restore
the original form, since romanization according to the Table may
result in a bizarre spelling. Thus *Milwaukee* transcribed into Hebrew is מילווקי; reromanized according to the rules it would come
out *Milvoki*. Similarly, Washington would become *Vashington*; *Cincinnati, Sinsinati; New Orleans--Nyu Orlins; Chevrolet--Shevroleh;
Marseilles--Marsei; Air France--Er Frans* (the vocalization being
supplied where Hebrew does not show it). Even more than geographical names, the romanizer may want to restore personal names to
their original spelling, if he recognizes them in their Hebrew
transcription and knows their exact individual spelling (*Shechter,*

Schächter; Wiener, Weiner, Veaner?)[16] Sometimes, names other than English or possibly German, can really puzzle the English romanizer (רנו-Renault!), and he has no choice but to transliterate what he sees and add a question mark (*rnv?*). However, the romanizer is free to romanize also proper nouns according to the rules, if he so wishes.

(2) Foreign or international words in Hebrew other than proper nouns whose pronunciation is the same as in English, may be romanized according to the rules or rendered in their English spelling. This depends on context or emphasis or the intention of the romanizer. Examples are: *instinkt (instinct), paradoks (paradox), pesimizm (pessimism), telefon (telephone), sleng (slang), panter (panther), fantom (phantom), ekzost (exhaust), fyuz (fuse), rendvu (rendez-vous)*. Seeing that such words in Hebrew context may well be considered Hebrew words, and seeing further that not all of them have entered Hebrew from English, the romanizer will often prefer romanization to rendering them in English spelling. But when the foreign character of such words stands clearly out, as in היברו יוניון קולג' (Hebrew Union College), "פייס דה ניישן" ("Face The Nation") or אסושיאיטד פרס (Associated Press), rendering the original spelling seems the sensible thing to do.

(3) Modern Hebrew has added to its alphabet three characters for the foreign sounds /ğ/, /z̆/ and /c̆/, as found at the beginning of the names *George, Jacques* (French pronunciation) and *Chester.*[17] They are apostrophed ג, ז and צ respectively, thus ג׳, ז׳ and צ׳ (the apostrophe may also be found to be curved slanting and sometimes straight; ג׳ or ג'). Now these characters can of course be romanized by taking over the apostrophe together with the basic letter, thus *g', z'* and *ts'*. However, such a romanization can be confusing, because the apostrophe is used in this romanization to take the place of Hebrew *alef* and *ayin* in certain positions (see above, page 20).

Faced with romanizations like *pig'amah* (פיג׳מה 'pyjama') and *pig'e* (פגעי 'afflictions of'), *mits'el* (מיצ׳ל 'Mitchell') and *mits'ad* (מצעד 'march') or *maz'ino* (מז׳ינו 'Maginot') and *maz'ek* (מזעק 'alarm bell'), a reader may not know whether to read *g', z'* and *ts'* as /ğ/, /z̆/ and /c̆/ or as simple *g, z* and *ts*.

It is, therefore, better to avoid the romanizations *g', z'* and *ts'*, if possible. If ג׳, ז׳ or צ׳ occur in proper nouns, the ro-

manizer may at any rate prefer restoring the original, as in (1).
Thus he will render ג'ונסון - *Johnson*, יוג'ין - *Eugene*, דון ז'ואן -
Don Juan, מירז' - *Mirage*, צ'ירצ'יל - *Churchill*.

   In common words, he may likewise want to restore the original,
provided that the pronunciation has not changed in Hebrew and that
his context permits it. Examples are: קוטג' - *cottage*, פריג'ידר -
Frigidaire, פיג'ין - *Pidgin* (English), ג'יפ - *jeep* (plural *jeepim*),
צ'יפס - *chips*, קלץ' - *clutch*, סנדויץ' - *sandwich*, טץ'-ווד - *touch-
wood* (and the following occurring in Hebrew in French pronunciation), ז'ורנל - *journal*, ז'רגון - *jargon*, ז'קט - *jacket* (or perhaps
jaquette), ביז' - *beige*.

   When words containing one of the three characters have changed
pronunciation in Hebrew or are foreign to English the romanizer can
avoid using *g'*, *z'* and *ts'* by writing a reasonable phonetic rendition of the word, e.g., ג'ינג'י ('redhead' from 'ginger') - *gingi*,
פנצ'ר ('accident' from 'puncture') - *punsher*, ספונג'ה ('wetmop',
cf. 'sponge', via Ladino) - *sponja*, פינג'ן ('coffee pot' from
Arabic) - *finjan*.[18]

   (4) If a foreign or international word has been hebraized by
the addition of a Hebrew morpheme or by any change whatever, one
should romanize such words rather than write their English equivalents. Examples are: *universitah, televizyah, informatsyah, para-
doksim, inteligenti, formali, fantasti, monote'izm, antishemiut,
relevantiut*. There may be occasions, when the equivalent is preferable, e.g., *America* instead of *Amerikah*, or *Europe* instead of
Europah. But one must carefully weigh the situation, realizing that
America and *Europe* are really *translations* rather than romanizations of the hebraized (and therefore Hebrew) forms.

   (5) If foreign or international words are more completely hebraized, so that they appear in Hebrew grammatical patterns, they can
only be romanized, e.g., *tilfen* 'to telephone', *tsitet* 'to quote'
(cite), *kitlug* 'cataloguing', *mefustar* 'Pasteurized'.

   (6) Loanwords from earlier periods that have assumed a distinct
Hebrew form must likewise be romanized, e.g., *teatron, himnon,
signon, kartis, prozdor, aklim, mekatreg, itstadyon, kuntres*.

   (7) Proper nouns that possess a distinct form in Hebrew, e.g.,
Atunah (Athens), *Kushta* (Constantinople), *Luv* (Lybia), *Aflaton*
(Plato) will normally be romanized. If the romanizer, in a certain
context or because the word occurs in isolation, prefers to write

the form familiar to English readers, he must realize that, this
would again mean a translation rather than a romanization.

(8) A special case is formed by non-English foreign names like
מינכן or קלן, in which an original sound (here German ü and ö) is
rendered in Hebrew by the nearest equivalent. The romanizer may
then well be in a quandary whether to write *Minchen* and *Keln* or the
original *München* and *Köln* (the English equivalents *Munich* and
Cologne would, again, represent translations).

(9) Colloquial and slang words stemming from foreign words (and
not containing the נ‎, ז‎, צ‎, letters; see above, 3) must be romanized (i.e., one should not attempt to restore the original form),
e.g., *blondini*, *sveder* (sweater), *mesting* (mess tin), *trempist*
(from tramp-hitchhike).

(10) Yiddish words in Hebrew text must be romanized according to
the rules for romanizing Hebrew and not those for romanizing Yiddish (which are different; see below, page 44). Examples are:
chochmeh, *chochmes*,[19] *chevrehman*, *kuntsim*, *shnor*, *tsimes*, *shvitser*,
alte zachen, *shmates*, *aizen*.

(11) Words borrowed by Hebrew from a language using a non-Latin
alphabet (Cyrillic, Arabic, etc.) should be romanized the way they
are written when they are romanized in English directly from the
original language, e.g., *Khrushchev*, *Zhitomir*, *Nasser*, *Baghdad*,
jiujitsu.

(12) All previous cases dealt with foreign or international
words in Hebrew. Now there is also a category of Hebrew words,
which possess one or several internationally conventionalized forms,
e.g., *Jerusalem*, *Zion*, *Gaza*, *Bethlehem*, *Tiberias*, *Safed* or *Isaac*,
Jacob, *Moses*. When the romanizer comes upon one of these, he must
be sure to romanize them according to the rules; thus: *Yerushalayim*,
Tsiyon, *Azah*, *Bet Lechem*, *Tveryah*, *Tsfat* (or *Tsefat*), *Yitschak*;
Yaakov (or *Ya'akov*), *Mosheh*. When the text intentionally renders
the English pronunciation of such words, e.g., ג׳רוסלם פוסט (Jerusalem Post) or ג׳ייקובס (Jacobs), the romanizer will want to restore the English spelling (rather than romanizing these words;
see above, 1).

Annotated Samples

Syllabification of words by hyphen goes a long way in helping a
reader to pronounce a Hebrew word correctly. It is indicated with

beginning students and with people who know little or no Hebrew. It is especially useful in songs, prayers and any solemn or formal reading.

Unhyphenated romanization, on the other hand, saves space, is easier to write or type and conveys the impression of regular words rather than loose syllables.

Kadish *(syllabified)*[20]

Yit-ga-dal ve-yit-ka-dash shmeh ra-ba, be-al-ma di vra chir-u-teh, ve-yam-lich mal-chu-teh, be-cha-ye-chon uv-yo-me-chon uv-cha-ye de-chol Bet Yis-ra-el, ba-a-ga-la u-viz-man ka-riv, ve-im-ru a-men.

Ye-he shmeh ra-ba me-va-rach, le-a-lam ul-al-me almaya.

Yit-ba-rach ve-yish-ta-bach ve-yit-pa-ar ve-yit-ro-mam ve-yit-na-se, ve-yit-ha-dar ve-yit-a-leh ve-yit-ha-lal shmeh de-kud-sha brich hu, le-e-la min kol bir-cha-ta ve-shi-ra-ta, tush-be-cha-ta ve-ne-che-ma-ta, da-a-mi-ran be-al-ma, ve-im-ru a-men.

Ye-he shla-ma ra-ba min shma-ya ve-cha-yim, a-le-nu ve-al kol Yis-ra-el, ve-im-ru a-men.

O-seh sha-lom bim-ro-mav, hu ya-a-seh sha-lom a-le-nu ve-al kol Yis-ra-el, ve-im-ru a-men.

Remarks

(1) The high incidence of the ending -*a* rather than -*ah* is due to the Aramaic ending אָ.

(2) The use of commas is based upon one common phrasing in the recital of the prayer. A romanizer may change the phrasing or he may want to arrange the *Kadish* in lines, each of which begins with a capital letter, e.g.:

Yit-ga-dal . . .

Be-al-ma . . .

Be-cha-ye-chon . . .

Ba-a-ga-la . . ., etc.

(3) Option of rendering *tsere ei* instead of *e*. At the end of a word in: *shmeih, chir-u-teih, mal-chu-teih, uv-cha-yei, Ye-hei, ul-al-mei* and *ve-yit-na-sei* (but note that the vowel in *ve-yit-a-leh, O-seh* and *ya-a-seh* is *segol* and not *tsere*). Less desirable, but permitted would be *ei* for *tsere* also in the middle of the word in: *be-cha-yei-chon, uv-yo-mei-chon, a-mein, Beit, le-eila* and *a-lei-nu*.

(4) Option of rendering *shva* in: *she-meh, ve-ra, u-ve-yo-me-chon, u-ve-cha-ye, u-le-al-me* and *be-rich* (the *ei* option for *tsere* may be added, e.g., *she-meih*). Rendition of *shva* in *u-viz-man, ve-im-ru* and *bim-ro-mav* is not recommended.

Kadish *(not syllabified)*

Yitgadal veyitkadash shmeh raba, be'alma di vra chiruteh, veyam-lich malchuteh, bechayechon uvyomechon uvchaye dechol Bet Yisrael, baagala uvizman kariv, ve'imru amen.

Yehe shmeh raba mevarach le'alam ulalme almaya.

Yitbarach veyishtabach veyitpaar veyitromam veyitnase, veyitha-dar veyitaleh veyithalal shmeh dekudsha brich hu, le'ela min kol birchata veshirata, tushbechata venechemata, daamiran be'alma, ve'-imru amen.

Yehe shlama raba min shmaya vechayim, alenu ve'al kol Yisrael, ve'imru amen.

Oseh shalom bimromav, hu yaaseh shalom alenu ve'al kol Yisrael, ve'imru amen.

Remarks

(1) 1-4 of the syllabified version are valid here too.

(2) Due to the absence of syllabification, an apostrophe is used as an intervocalic separation with the groups *ea (le'alam, be'alma, ve'al), ee (le'ela)* and *ei (ve'imru)*. It may further be used with *aa (ba'agala, veyitpa'ar, da'amiran, ya'aseh)* and in a post-conso-nantal position: *chir'uteh, ul'alme, veyit'aleh*

(3) The *th* group may be separated by apostrophe in *vehit'hadar* and *veyit'halal*.

Kadish *(Ashkenazic, not syllabified)*

Yisgadal veyiskadash shmeih rabo, be'olmo di vro chiruseih, veyamlich malchuseih, bechayeichon, uvyomeichon uvchayei dechol Beis Yisroeil, baagolo uvizman koriv, ve'imru omein.

Yehei shmeih rabo mevorach le'olam ulolmei olmayo.

Yisborach veyishtabach veyispoar veyisromam veyisnasei, veyis-hadar veyisaleh veyishalal shmeih dekudsho brich hu, le'eilo min kol birchoso veshiroso, tushbechoso venechemoso, daamiron be'olmo ve'imru omein.

Yehei shlomo rabo min shmayo vechayim, oleinu ve'al kol Yisroeil, ve'imru omein.

Oseh sholom bimromov, hu yaaseh sholom oleinu ve'al kol Yisroeil, ve'imru omein.

Remarks

(1) The remarks for the Sephardic version are valid here too, except that the ending ‏אָ‎ results in -o and that in *veyis'hadar* and *veyis'halal* it is *sh* rather than *th* that may be broken up by apostrophe.

(2) The *ei* option has been chosen because the diphthongal pronunciation of *tsere* is preferred in Ashkenazic.

(3) The *ou* option for *cholam* would result in: *bechayeichoun, uvyoumeichoun, veyisroumom, ouseh sholoum bimroumov.*

Ve'ahavta *(syllabified)*

Ve-a-hav-ta et A-do-nai E-lo-he-cha be-chol le-vav-cha uv-chol naf-she-cha uv-chol me-o-de-cha. Ve-ha-yu had-va-rim ha-e-leh a-sher a-no-chi me-tsav-cha ha-yom al le-va-ve-cha. Ve-shi-nan-tam le-va-ne-cha ve-di-bar-ta bam be-shiv-te-cha be-ve-te-cha uv-lech-te-cha va-de-rech uv-shoch-be-cha uv-ku-me-cha. Uk-shar-tam le-ot al ya-de-cha ve-ha-yu le-to-ta-fot ben e-ne-cha. Uch-tav-tam al me-zu-zot be-te-cha u-vish-a-re-cha.

Remarks

(1) In *naf-she-cha* the *e* stands for *shva* while in *me-o-dê-cha* it stands for stressed *segol*. By analogy, readers may incorrectly read *naf-shê-cha*. Similarly, the *e* in *be-shiv-te-cha* may be stressed on the analogy of *be-ve-têcha* and the one in *uv-shoch-be-cha* on the analogy of *uv-ku-mê-cha*. The remedy for such errors is frequent congregational recital.

(2) Options: *ei* instead of *e* for *tsere*: at the end of a word: none. In the middle of a word, in: *eit* (here pointed with *tsere*), *ha-ei-leh, be-vei-te-cha, bein, ei-ne-cha, bei-te-cha.* Rendering *shva* (of special significance since this is a Torah text) in: *le-va-ve-cha, u-ve-chol, ha-de-va-rim, me-tsa-ve-cha, u-ve-lech-te-cha u-ve-shoch-be-cha, u-ve-ku-me-cha, U-ke-shar-tam, u-che-tav-tam.*

(3) When the option of these *shvas* is chosen, *le-va-ve-cha* and *me-tsa-ve-cha* add to the possible errors of stressing the *e* in analogy to other words.

(4) According to some grammarians the *shva* after initial *u-* is not really a vocal *shva*, however it is customary to pronounce them in formal recitation or chanting.

Ve'ahavta *(not syllabified)*

Ve'ahavta et Adonai Elohecha bechol levavcha uvchol nafshecha
uvchol me'odecha. Vehayu hadvarim ha'eleh asher anochi metsavcha
hayom al levavecha. Veshinantam levanecha vedibarta bam beshivtecha
bevetecha uvlechtecha vaderech uvshochbecha uvkumecha. Ukshartam
le'ot al yadecha vehayu letotafot ben enecha. Uchtavtam al mezuzot
betecha uvish'arecha.

Remarks

(1) 1-4 of the syllabified version apply.

(2) Apostrophe between *ea* and *eo* and, post-consonantally in
uvish'arecha.

Hatikvah *(syllabified)*

Kol od ba-le-vav pni-mah

Ne-fesh ye-hu-di ho-mi-yah

Ul-fa-a-te miz-rach ka-di-mah

A-yin Le-tsi-yon tso-fi-yah

Od lo av-dah tik-va-te-nu

Ha-tik-vah shnot al-pa-yim

Lih-yot am chof-shi be-ar-tse-nu

Be-e-rets Tsi-yon Vi-ru-sha-la-yim.

Remarks

(1) The silent *h* at the end of the syllable in *lih-yot* is rendered in analogy to the *-ah* and *-eh* endings.

(2) Options: *ei* instead of *e* at the end of the word, in *Ul-fa-
a-tei*; in the middle of the word, in *ba-lei-vav, tik-va-tei-nu, be-
ar-tsei-nu.* Rendering *shva* in *pe-ni-mah, U-le-fa-a-te, she-not, li-
he-yot.*

(3) Vocal *shva* in *li-he-yot* is grammatically incorrect but is
required by the melody in some syllabifications. Grammatically,
there might be a *shva* in *av-dah (a-ve-dah)*, but the melody excludes it.

(4) The rendition *vi-Ye-ru-sha-la-yim* is incorrect. ו preceded
by /i/ becomes silent.

(5) As regards punctuation the romanizer will go by commas and
periods in his original Hebrew text.

Hatikvah *(not syllabified)*

Kol od balevav pnimah

Nefesh yehudi homiyah

Ulfa'ate mizrach kadimah

Ayin Letsiyon tsofiyah

Od lo avdah tikvatenu

Hatikvah shnot alpayim

Lihyot am chofshi be'artsenu

Be'erets Tsiyon Virushalayim

Remarks

(1) 1-4 of the syllabified version apply.

(2) Apostrophe between *aa, ea* and *ee.*

Maoz Tsur *(not syllabified)*

Maoz tsur yeshuati lecha na'eh leshabe'ach

Tikon bet tefilati vesham todah nezabe'ach

Le'et tachin matbe'ach mitsar hamnabe'ach

Az egmor beshir mizmor chanukat hamizbe'ach.

Yevanim nikbetsu alai azai bime Chashmanim

Ufartsu chomot migdalai vetimu kol hashmanim

Uminotar kankanim naasah nes leshoshanim

Bene binah yeme shmonah kavu shir urnanim.

Remarks

(1) Optional *ei* instead of *e* for *tsere* at the end of the word
in: *bimei, Benei, yemei;* in the middle of the words in: *beit, le'eit*
and *leshabei'ach* with its four rhyming words. These longer words
might also profitably be written with *ế*, because it tells the
reader which syllable to stress, thus *leshabếach*, etc. The apostrophe is then unnecessary.

(2) Post-consonantal *alef* and *ayin*, respectively, may be expressed in *vetim'u* and *kav'u* to achieve correct syllabification.

(3) *Maoz* and *yeshuati* do not need an intervocalic apostrophe. In
na'aseh it is optional.

(4) If a romanizer does not recognize *Chashmanim* as a proper
noun and fails to capitalize it, not much damage has been done. So
also with other capitalized words in these samples.

(5) *Bime* is like *Virushalayim* in the *Hatikvah; biyeme* is incorrect.

(6) For a syllabification consider the apostrophes in the present version as well as points 3 and 4 of the Remarks. There should
be no difficulty.

Yerushalayim Shel Zahav *(not syllabified)*

Avir harim tsalul kayayin vere'ach oranim

Nisa beruach haarbayim im kol paamonim

Uvtardemat ilan va'even shvuyah bachalomah

Ha'ir asher badad yoshevet uvelibah chomah.

Yerushalayim shel zahav veshel nechoshet veshel or

Halo lechol shirayich ani kinor.

Remarks

(1) Optional apostrophe in *ha'arbayim* and *pa'amonim*.

(2) The absence of *e* for *shva* in *Uvtardemat* and *shvuyah* and its presence in *uvelibah* follows the syllable requirement of the melody.

A Hebrew Lesson *(not syllabified)*

Shalom gveret. Hizmanti cheder al shem Yakov Weinstein.
Lehayom?

Ken. Cheder im telefon ve'ambatyah.

Lishnayim?

Ken, shte mitot. Ishti bachuts im hamitan.

Beseder gamur. Bvakashah leherashem.

Mah hamchir leyom?

Shivim veshesh lirot kolel aruchat boker.

Ha'im zeh kolel sherut?

Lo adoni. Yesh tsorech lehosif chamishah asar achuz. Kamah zman tish-hu?

Remarks

(1) If the text is unpointed, only a person with a good knowledge of Hebrew can romanize it.

(2) For spoken Hebrew the consonant clusters in *gveret, bvakashah, zman* are likely to be preferred to inserting a *shva*. In *hamechir* it can be added optionally.

(3) The *ei* option may be chosen at the end of a word, *shtei* and --unnecessarily-- inside the word in an open syllable, *leheirashem*. It would not be used in *shem, ken, shesh, yesh, kolel*.

(4) Intervocalic apostrophe in *ve'ambatyah* and *ha'im*.

(5) Option of postconsonantal apostrophe in *mit'an* and *shiv'im*.

(6) *Lishnayim* is the grammatical form. In the speech of many it will sound *leshnayim*, and the romanizer might have chosen that pronunciation.

(7) The word *tish-hu* is syllabified to avoid the puzzling cluster *shh*.

(8) Regarding *Yakov:* The romanizer chooses this form (or *Ya'akov*) if his text has the Hebrew form, יעקב. Should it have ג'ייקוב he will write *Jacob*.

(9) Regarding *Weinstein:* The name may appear in Hebrew with one or two *yods*, possibly also with two *vavs*. It cannot be romanized mechanically. The personal spelling may be *Vainstein, Wajnsztajn,* etc. In choosing *Weinstein* the romanizer takes a guess based on one frequent spelling.

Concerning the Word Lists

(1) The General Word List contains approximately 500 words of relatively high frequency, in English alphabetical order. It is intended to help the romanizer with single words and expressions, not with transcribing continuous text.

(2) Following the General List are seven Special Lists:

The Alphabet

The Vowel Points

The Jewish Months

Holidays, Festivals, Fasts

The Books of the Bible

The Weekly Torah Portions

The Mishnah or Talmud Tractates

Since words in these areas are not also contained in the General List the romanizer must look for them in the Special Lists.

(3) The spelling employed in the lists is proposed as the standard English spelling of these words. This does not exclude respelling words for special purposes according to the more exact romanization or a scientific transliteration.

(4) Spelling variants are indicated by *or;* they are based on the options discussed above. If an expression consists of several words, only the one containing the variant is repeated, e.g., *brit milah* or *berit*. Only one plural form is listed with several optional singular spellings. If the plural form is followed by "etc.," it means that the romanizer may supply the different plural forms corresponding with the singular options. E.g., the entry *brachah* or *Brachah* or *berachah* or *Berachah* plural *brachot*, etc. means that *Brachot, berachot* and *Berachot* are other possible plural forms. The

ei or *é* option for *tsere* is not used in the Word Lists; every *tsere* is rendered *e*. The final *h* is always rendered. The exceptional spellings with *tz* and doubled consonant are not used. However, the romanizer may use these options, as explained above. He may, furthermore, handle capitalization differently from the way it is listed, and he may occasionally want to insert an *e* for *shva* and an apostrophe as a syllable divider where these are not provided in the Lists--or to omit one that seems unnecessary.

(5) The entries are sometimes "corrective" as far as Hebrew grammar is concerned. Thus, for instance, the grammatical plural is listed where common usage has a yiddishized or anglicized one, e.g., *ame haarets*, *baale kriah* or *shochatim* instead of *am haratsim* (Yiddish *ameratsim*), *baal kriahs* and *shochtim*. In some cases, however, one of the latter forms is given because there is no good Hebrew form, e.g., *bar mitsvahs* (the ceremony), *brit milahs*. (The plural ending *-ahs* is not listed when the word has the normal Hebrew *-ot*; however, the context may cause a romanizer to use *-ahs* also with these words, especially when they are very common in English, e.g., *menorahs* instead of *menorot*). Finally, the List contains also some conventionalized ungrammatical forms, as for instance, *sidrot*.

(6) Words like *hosanna*, *Messiah*, *sabbath* or *shibboleth* are considered English loan words and, therefore, not included in the Word List. The same is true of *hallelujah* in that spelling. In the general-purpose romanization of Hebrew it would appear as *haleluyah*. The English spellings *Esther* and *Ruth* have been accepted as optional, together with the romanizations *Ester* and *Rut*. The word *amen* appears the same in English and in romanized Hebrew; but in the latter the *a* is pronounced "like in *father*."

(7) Another group of words, for which the romanizer may look in vain, is omitted in the List because they are Yiddish rather than Hebrew. Among such words, which are frequently used in Jewish context, are (romanization according to the system devised by the Yivo Institute for Jewish Research): *balebos*, *balegole*, *mayse*, *shabes-goy*, *sheygets*, *shiker*, *shikse*, *shlimazl*, *yortsayt*, *yarmlke* and Yiddish words for food items. Other words, known best in their Yiddish form, have been re-Hebraized, e.g., *chatunah (khasene) cheder (kheyder)*, *davka (dafka)*, *mishloach manot (shlakh-mones)*, *rachmanut (rakhmones)*, *tsarot (tsores)*. Still other words listed in

their Hebrew forms may well have come into English usage from Yiddish rather than directly from Hebrew. Among such words may be, e.g., *hekdesh, meshuga, sechel, yeshivah, yichus*.

(8) Names of organizations are listed in their own spelling, e.g., *Bezalel, B'nai B'rith, Hadassah*.

General Word List

Acharonim

Adir Hu

Adloyada

Adon

Adon Olam

Adonai

afikoman

agadah, *plural* agadot

agorah, *plural* agorot

Agudat Harabanim

Agudat Yisrael *also* Agudas
   Yisroel *also* Agudas Israel

agunah, *plural* agunot

Akedah

Akedat Yitschak

Al Chet

alav hashalom

alechem shalom

aleha hashalom

Alenu

aliyah, *plural* aliyot

am haarets *or* ha'arets, *plural*
   ame haarets

Amidah

Am Segulah

Amora, *plural* Amoraim *or*
   Amora'im

apikores, *plural* apikorsim

Aravah

arba kosot

arbaah banim

arbaah minim

aron hakodesh

Aseret Hadibrot

Aseret Yeme Hatshuvah *or* Hate-
   shuvah

Ashkenazi, *plural* Ashkenazim

atarah, *plural* atarot

avel, *plural* avelim

avelut

averah, *plural* averot

Avinu Malkenu

Avodah

Azazel

baal *or* Baal, *plural* be'alim
   also baalim

baal kriah *or* keriah, *plural*
   baale kriah, *etc.*

baal tefilah, *plural* baale
   tefilah

baal tekiah, *plural* baale tekiah

Baalshem

Baal Shem Tov

bar mitsvah, *plural* bar mitsvahs
   (ceremony), bene mitsvah
   (boys)

Barchu *or* Barechu

baruch haba, *plural* bruchim
   habaim *or* haba'im *or* beruchim

Baruch Hashem

bat mitsvah, *plural* bat mitsvahs
   (ceremony), benot mitsvah
   (girls)

bedikat chamets

beezrat Hashem *or* be'ezrat

besamim

beseder

bet din, *plural* bate din

bet (ha)midrash, *plural* bate
   (ha)midrash

Bet (Ha)mikdash

beteavon *or* bete'avon

betsah, *plural* betsim

bevakashah

Bezalel

bikur cholim

bimah

Birkat Hamazon

bitul chamets

biur chamets

bli neder

B'nai B'rith

boker tov

brachah *or* Brachah *or* berachah
  or Berachah, *plural* brachot,
  etc.

brachah levatalah

brit milah *or* berit, *plural* brit
  milahs·

chacham, *plural* chachamim

Chad Gadya

Chag Haasif *or* Ha'asif

Chag Habikurim

Chag Hakatsir

Chag Hamatsot

Chag Hashavuot

Chag Hasukot

chag sameach

chai

chalah, *plural* chalot

chalitsah

chalukah

chaluts, *plural* chalutsim

chalutsah, *plural* chalutsot

Chamesh Megilot

chamets

Chamishah Chumshe Torah

charoset

chas vechalilah

chas veshalom

chasid, *plural* chasidim

chasidut

chatan, *plural* chatanim

Chatan Bereshit

Chatan Torah

chatunah, *plural* chatunot

chavurah, *plural* chavurot

chazak

chazak chazak venitchazek

chazak veemats *or* ve'emats

chazan, *plural* chazanim

cheder, *plural* chadarim

cherem

Chevrah Kadisha

Chilul Hashem

chochmah

Chol Hamoed *or* Hamo'ed

Choshen Hamishpat

chumash *or* Chumash, *plural*
  chumashim

chupah, *plural* chupot

chutspah, *plural* chutspot

davka

dayan, *plural* dayanim

derech erets

din

Din Torah

drash

drashah *or* derashah, *plural*
  drashot, *etc.*

drush

echad

El Al

El Male Rachamim

Elohenu

Elohim

Emek (Yizreel *or* Yizre'el)

emet

En Kelohenu

Erets Yisrael

Erev *(followed by the name of
  the individual holy day)*

Erev Shabat

Erev Yom Tov

eruv, *plural* eruvim

etrog, *plural* etrogim

ets chayim, *plural* atse chayim

etsah, *plural* etsot

Even Haezer *or* Ha'ezer

ezrat nashim

gabai, *plural* gabaim *or* gaba'im

galut *or* Galut

Gan Eden

gaon *or* Gaon, *plural* geonim

gelilah

gemar chatimah tovah

gemar tov

Gemara

gematriah, *plural* gematriot

gemilut chesed, chasadim

genizah, *plural* genizot

ger, *plural* gerim

ger tsedek, *plural* gere tsedek

get

geulah *or* ge'ulah

goi, *plural* goyim

golah

Gveret *or* Geveret

Haarets *or* Ha'arets

hachnasat kalah

hachnasat orchim

hachsharah

Hadassah

hadlakat hanerot

haftarah, *plural* haftarot

Haftarat *(followed by the name of the individual haftarah)*

hagadah *or* Hagadah, *plural* hagadot, *etc.*

Hagadah Shel Pesach

Haganah

hagbahah

Hakadosh Baruch Hu

hakafah, *plural* hakafot

Hakotel Hamaaravi *or* Hama'aravi

halachah *or* Halachah, *plural* halachot

Halel

haleluyah

Hamotsi

Haskalah

Hatikvah

Havdalah

hechsher, *plural* hechsherim

hefker

hekdesh

heter

hifil *or* hif'il

Histadrut

hitpael *or* hitpa'el

hoshana, *plural* hoshanot

hufal *or* huf'al *also* hofal *or* hof'al

ilui, *plural* iluyim

Irgun

Isru Chag

isur, *plural* isurim

ivri

ivrit *or* Ivrit

Kabalah

Kabalat Shabat

Kadish

kahal

kal

kal vachomer

kalah

kaparah

karpas

kasher

kashrut

Kedushah

kehilah, *plural* kehilot

Kehilah Kedoshah (*followed by the name of the individual congregation*)

Kehilat Hakodesh (*followed by the name of the individual congregation*)

Keren Hayesod

Keren Kayemet Leyisrael

keter, *plural* ketarim

Keter Torah

ketivah vachatimah tovah

ketubah, *plural* ketubot

Ketuvim (*Bible Part*)

kevutsah, *plural* kevutsot

kezayit

kibud

kibuts, *plural* kibutsim

kibutsnik, *plural* kibutsnikim

Kidush

Kidush Hashem

kidushin

kinah *or* Kinah, *plural* kinot, etc.

kipah, *plural* kipot

Klal Yisrael *or* Kelal

Kneset *or* Keneset

Kohen, *plural* Kohanim

kol chatan vekol kalah

Kol Nidre

kol shofar, *plural* kolot shofar

kol tuv

Kol Yisrael

Kotel (Maaravi *or* Ma'aravi)

kriah *or* keriah

Kupat Cholim

labriut *also* livriut

lailah tov

Lechah Dodi

lechayim

lehitraot

lel menuchah

leolam vaed *or* le'olam va'ed

leshanah habaah Birushalayim *or* haba'ah

leshanah tovah tikatev(u)

leshon hakodesh

leshon hara *also* lashon

Levi, *plural* Leviyim

luach, *plural* luchot

lulav, *plural* lulavim

Maariv *or* Ma'ariv

maasim tovim *or* ma'asim

machzor *or* Machzor, *plural* machzorim

madrich, *plural* madrichim

maftir

Magen David

Magen David Adom

magid, *plural* magidim

Mah Nishtanah

mah shlomcha

Mah Tovu

malach *or* mal'ach, *plural* malachim, *etc.*

malach hamavet *or* mal'ach

Malchuyot

mamzer, *plural* mamzerim

maot chitim

Maoz Tsur

Mapai

Mapam

marit ayin *or* mar'it

maror

masechet *or* Masechet *also* masechta *or* Masechta, *plural* masechtot

mashgiach

Mashiach

maskil, *plural* maskilim

Masorah

matsah, *plural* matsot

matsah shmurah *or* shemurah

matsevah, *plural* matsevot

mazal

mazal tov

Mechilta

mechutan, *plural* mechutanim

Medinat Yisrael

Mefarshim

megilah *or* Megilah, *plural* megilot, *etc.*

Megilat Ester *or* Esther

Melaveh Malkah

menorah, *plural* menorot

menuchah

meshuga

meshulach, *plural* meshulachim

metsiah, *plural* metsiot

mezuzah, *plural* mezuzot

midrash *or* Midrash, *plural* midrashim, *etc.*

mikveh, *plural* mikvot

milah

Minchah

minhag, *plural* minhagim

minyan, *plural* minyanim

Misheberach

mishloach manot

mishnah *or* Mishnah, *plural* mishnayot *or* Mishnahs

Mishneh Torah

mitnaged, *plural* mitnagdim

mitsvah, *plural* mitsvot

mizrach *or* Mizrach

Mizrachi

moadim lesimchah *or* mo'adim

Modim Anachnu Lach

moed *or* mo'ed, *plural* moadim *or* mo'adim

mohel, *plural* mohalim

morah, *plural* morot

moreh, *plural* morim

Moreh Nevuchim

moshav, *plural* moshavim

moshavah, *plural* moshavot

Mosheh Rabenu

Motsa'e Shabat

Motsa'e Yom Tov

Musaf

nagid, *plural* negidim

nasi *or* Nasi, *plural* nesiim

navi *or* Navi, *plural* neviim

nedavah, *plural* nedavot

neder, *plural* nedarim

Negev

Ne'ilah

nekamah, *plural* nekamot

ner tamid

nes gadol hayah sham

neshamah, *plural* neshamot

Neviim

Neviim Acharonim

Neviim Rishonim

nifal *or* nif'al

nigun, *plural* nigunim

nusach, *plural* nusachim

olah, *plural* olot

olah chadashah, *plural* olot chadashot

olam haba

olam hazeh

oleh, *plural* olim

oleh chadash, *plural* olim chadashim

Omer

Oneg Shabat, *plural* Onge Shabat

Orach Chayim

Palmach

panim

parashah, *plural* parashot *also* parashiot

Parashat *(followed by the name of the individual parashah)*

parashat hashavua, *plural* parashot hashavua

parnas, *plural* parnasim

parochet, *plural* parochot

pasul

pe'ah, *plural* pe'ot

perush *or* Perush, *plural* perushim, *etc.*

petichah

pidyon haben

piel *or* pi'el

pikuach nefesh

pilpul, *plural* pilpulim

Pirke Avot

piyut, *plural* piyutim

Poskim

pual *or* pu'al

Raban

Rabenu

rabotai

rachmanut

rav *or* Rav, *plural* rabanim

refuah shlemah

Resh Galuta

Ribono Shel Olam

rimon, *plural* rimonim

Rishonim

Rosh Chodesh

Rosh Yeshivah

ruach hakodesh

sabra, *plural* sabras

sandak, *plural* sandakim

sanhedrin

sechel

Seder, *plural* Sedarim

Sefer Torah, *plural* Sifre Torah

Sefirah

Sefirat Haomer *or* Ha'omer

selichah *or* Selichah, *plural* selichot, *etc.*

Sephardi, *plural* Sephardim

se'udah, *plural* se'udot

se'udat mitsvah, *plural* se'udot mitsvah

Se'udah Shlishit

Shabat, *plural* Shabatot

Shabat Breshit *or* Bereshit

Shabat Chazon

Shabat Chol Hamoed

Shabat Hachodesh

Shabat Hagadol

Shabat Mevarchim

Shabat Nachamu

Shabat Parah

shabat shalom

Shabat Shekalim

Shabat Shirah

Shabat Shuvah

Shabat Zachor

Shacharit

shadchan, *plural* shadchanim

shaliach, *plural* shlichim *or* shelichim

shalom

shalom alechem

Shalosh Regalim

Shalosh Se'udot

shamash, *plural* shamashim

sharav

shavua tov

Shechinah

shechitah

Shehecheyanu

shekel, *plural* shekalim

sheker

sheket

Shevarim

shiduch

shikun, *plural* shikunim

shiur, *plural* shiurim

shivah *or* shiv'ah

shliach tsibur *or* sheliach

shloshim *or* sheloshim

Shma (Yisrael) *or* Shema

shmitah *or* Shemitah

Shmoneh Esreh

shochet, *plural* shochatim

shofar, *plural* shofarot

Shofarot

Shulchan Aruch

shva

sidrah, *plural* sidrot

sidrat hashavua

sidur *or* Sidur, *plural* sidurim

simchah, *plural* simchot

siyum, *plural* siyumim

Sochnut

sofer, *plural* sofrim

sofer stam

Sofrim

sukah, *plural* sukot

taanit (tsibur) *or* ta'anit

talit, *plural* talitot, taliyot

talmid chacham, *plural* talmide
  chachamim

Talmud

Talmud Torah *(school)*

talmud torah *(study)*

Tana, *plural* Tanaim *or* Tana'im

Tanach

targum *or* Targum, *plural*
  targumim, *etc.*

tashlich

techiyat hametim

tefilah *or* Tefilah, *plural*
  tefilot, *etc.*

tefilin

tehilim

Tekiah

tenaim *or* tnaim *or* tena'im *or*
  tna'im

Teruah

teshuvah

Tikun (Chatsot, Lel Shavuot,
  Sofrim)

titchadesh, *feminine* titchadshi

Tnuvah *or* Tenuvah

todah (rabah)

tohorah *also* taharah

tohuvavohu

Torah

Torah Umesorah

Tosafot

Tosefta

totseret haarets

trefah

tsadik *or* Tsadik, *plural*
  tsadikim

Tsahal

tsarah, *plural* tsarot

tsedakah

tsitsit

Tsiyon

ulpan *or* Ulpan, *plural* ulpanim

Unetaneh Tokef

Vaad Arba Aratsot

Vaad Ha'ir

Vaad Halashon

yad, *plural* yadot *(pointer)*

Yad Vashem

Yamim Noraim *or* Nora'im

Yekum Purkan

Yerushalayim

yeshivah *or* Yeshivah, *plural*
  yeshivot

yetser hara

yetser hatov

yichus

Yigdal

yishar kochacha *or* koach

yishuv

Yisrael

yizkor

Yom Hadin

yom tov *or* Yom Tov, *plural* yamim
  tovim, *etc.*

Yom Truah *or* Teruah

Yoreh Deah *or* De'ah

yovel *or* Yovel

Zeman Cherutenu

Zeman Matan Toratenu

Zeman Simchatenu

zemirot

zeroa *or* zero'a, *plural* zeroot
  or zero'ot

Zichronot

Zim

Zohar

Special Word Lists

The Alphabet
alef
bet
vet
gimel
dalet
he
vav
zayin
chet
tet
yud *also* yod
kaf
chaf
lamed
mem
nun
samech
ayin
pe
fe
tsade *also* tsadi *also* tsadik
kuf *also* kof
resh
shin
tav

The Vowel Points
kamats (katan)
patach
tsere
segol
chirik (gadol)
cholam (chaser, male)
shuruk
kubuts

The Jewish Months
Nisan
Iyar
Sivan
Tamuz
Av
Elul
Tishri
Cheshvan *also* Marcheshvan
Kislev
Tevet
Shvat *or* Shevat
Adar
Adar Rishon *also* Adar Alef
Adar Sheni *also* Adar Bet *also* Veadar *or* Ve'adar

Holidays, Festivals, Fasts (*in chronological order. See General List for the special shabatot*)

Rosh Hashanah
Tsom Gedalyah
Yom Kipur
Sukot
Hoshana Raba
Shmini Atseret *or* Shemini
Simchat Torah
Chanukah
Asarah Betevet
Tu Bishvat *also* Chamishah Asar Bishvat
Taanit Ester *or* Ta'anit *or* Esther
Purim
Shushan Purim
Pesach
Yom Hashoah *or* Hasho'ah
Yom Hazikaron
Yom Haatsmaut *or* Haatsma'ut *or* Ha'atsma'ut

Lag Baomer *or* Ba'omer
Shavuot
Shivah Asar Betamuz *or* Shiv'ah
Tishah Beav *or* Tish'ah *or* Be'av
Chamishah Asar Beav *or* Be'av

The Books of the Bible
   Chumash:
Breshit *or* Bereshit
Shmot *or* Shemot
Vayikra
Bamidbar
Dvarim *or* Devarim
   Neviim Rishonim:
Yehoshua
Shoftim
Shmuel *or* Shemuel (Alef, Bet)
Melachim (Alef, Bet)
   Neviim Acharonim:
Yeshayahu
Yirmeyahu
Yechezkel
Hoshea
Yoel
Amos
Ovadyah
Yonah
Michah
Nachum
Chavakuk
Tsefanyah
Chagai
Zecharyah
Malachi *or* Mal'achi
   Ketuvim:
Tehilim
Mishle
Iyov
Shir Hashirim

Rut *or* Ruth
Echah
Kohelet
Ester *or* Esther
Daniel
Ezra
Nechemyah
Divre Hayamim (Alef, Bet)

The Weekly Torah Portions
Breshit *or* Bereshit
Noach
Lech Lecha
Vayera
Chaye Sarah
Toldot *also* Toledot
Vayetse
Vayishlach
Vayeshev
Mikets
Vayigash
Vayechi
Shmot *or* Shemot
Vaera *or* Va'era
Bo
Beshalach
Yitro
Mishpatim
Trumah *or* Terumah
Tetsaveh
Ki Tisa
Vayakhel *or* Vayak'hel
Pekude
Vayikra
Tsav
Shmini *or* Shemini
Tazria
Metsora
Achare Mot

Kedoshim

Emor

Behar

Bechukotai

Bamidbar

Naso

Behaalotcha *or* Beha'alotcha *also*
  Behaalotecha *or* Beha'alotecha

Shlach Lecha *or* Shelach

Korach

Chukat

Balak

Pinchas

Matot

Mase *or* Mas'e

Dvarim *or* Devarim

Vaetchanan *or* Va'etchanan

Ekev

Reeh *or* Re'eh

Shoftim

Ki Tetse

Ki Tavo

Nitsavim

Vayelech

Haazinu *or* Ha'azinu

Vezot Habrachah *or* Haberachah

The Mishnah or Talmud Tractates

   Seder Zeraim *or* Zera'im:

Brachot *or* Berachot

Peah *or* Pe'ah

Demai

Kilayim *or* Kil'ayim

Shviit *or* Sheviit *or* Shvi'it *or*
  Shevi'it

Trumot *or* Terumot

Maasrot *or* Ma'asrot

Maaser Sheni *or* Ma'aser

Chalah

Orlah

Bikurim

   Seder Moed *or* Mo'ed:

Shabat

Eruvin

Pesachim

Shekalim

Yoma

Sukah

Betsah *also* Yom Tov

Rosh Hashanah

Taanit *or* Ta'anit

Megilah

Moed Katan *or* Mo'ed

Chagigah

   Seder Nashim:

Yevamot

Ketubot

Nedarim

Nazir

Sotah

Gitin

Kidushin

   Seder Nesikin:

Baba Kama

Baba Metsia *or* Metsi'a

Baba Batra

Sanhedrin

Makot

Shvuot *or* Shevuot

Eduyot

Avodah Zarah

Avot

Horayot

   Seder Kodashim:

Zevachim

Menachot

Chulin

Bechorot

Arachin

Temurah

Kritot *or* Keritot

Meilah *or* Me'ilah

Tamid

Midot

Kinim

   Seder Tohorot:

Kelim

Oholot

Negaim *or* Nega'im

Parah

Tohorot *also* Teharot

Mikvaot

Nidah

Machshirin

Zavim

Tevul Yom

Yadayim

Okatsim *also* Oktsim *or* Okatsin
   or Oktsin *also* Uktsin

English word are limited to family names beginning with *Mac, O',
Van, La, De* and the like.

(15) The term *Ashkenazic*, like *Sephardic*, comprises a whole group
of pronunciations. For details see the article quoted in footnote 6.
In this booklet we speak about the pronunciation heard in most
American synagogues that use Ashkenazic.

(16) The catalogue of the HUC-JIR Library in Cincinnati shows no
less than twenty-three variant spellings of the name *Lifshits-
Lipshits*! - If the romanizer can read a name, but does not know its
spelling, he may have to romanize it according to the rules, adding
a question mark.

(17) The sound /ž/ is heard from many speakers also in originally
Hebrew words, when שׁ comes before a voiced consonant, e.g., in
חושבון *chežbon* or משגיח *mažgiach*. But it is always written שׁ.

(18) In a more exact romanization and even more so in a scientific
transliteration one may have to romanize ג׳, ז׳ and צ׳ according to
the respective rules rather than restore the original form. In
older texts, and occasionally also in contemporary ones, the three
sounds are written דזש, זש and טש respectively. These may likewise
have to be transliterated in a more exact romanization or a narrow
transliteration, while in the General-Purpose romanization they
are treated like ג׳, ז׳ and צ׳ with regard to romanization or res-
toration of the original.

(19) Such words are clearly marked in the Hebrew text, e.g. חכְמָה
instead of חכמה or חכְמַס or חכמה׳ס instead of חכמות.

(20) The *Kadish*, even though Aramaic rather than Hebrew, is included here because it is one of the most frequently romanized
prayers.